Stop Screwing Around

and

FORMAT Your Screenplay Like a PRO

Your Step-by-step Guide to
Formatting Your Screenplay to
Professional
Industry Standards

by
Robert L. McCullough

Second Printing Edition 2023

This book is written in Microsoft Word using
Courier Screenwriter, the standard font in use throughout
the film and television industry.

Also by the author:

Stop Screwing Around and *WIN*
Your Next Screenplay Contest

Stop Screwing Around and Write a
Screenplay that SELLS

The Hollywood Screenwriter:
An Insider's Guide to Professional Screenwriting

Screenwriting: The Theory and the Practice

Where Hollywood Hides: Celebrities in Paradise
(co-author Suzanne Herrera-McCullough)

Money for Your Movie: Guaranteed
(co-author Mark Stouffer, DGA)

Butterfly Beach Media Inc.
1187 Coast Village Rd. Ste. 512
Santa Barbara, Ca. 93108

Table of Contents

Seriously.
Who Cares?

You bought this book because you've either written a script that somehow doesn't look quite "right" or there are passages that for one reason or another just don't read very clearly...or you've got a killer idea for a movie or TV show but when you look at any script with all those capital letters and weird indentations and margins...maybe they just don't make a lot of sense at first glance.

But you're a writer and you've got an amazing story, complex and compelling characters with unpredictable plot turns and action sequences that could well redefine movies or television from this moment forward...so why not let someone else worry about all those weird margins and capitalizations and punctuations and stuff?

After all, how your script "looks" isn't really the point when you've got everything else going for it...right?

WRONG.

How your script looks—which is determined by adherence to specific formatting guidelines—sends a clear message to any manager, agent, producer, development executive, or reader at any reputable screenplay competition. The mere appearance of the words on your script pages immediately tells the world that you have at least a clue about the fundamentals of professional screenwriting. Ignore certain guidelines by deviating from industry standard formatting, and readers will mark you as a rank amateur well before they come to understand what a brilliant story you've written.

It all starts on Page One.

If the first few pages of your script are littered with spelling, or grammar errors (you really *should* understand the difference between "it's" and "its" and between "they're" and "their"), even the unpaid interns most screenplay

2

contests pass off as "reader" will promptly focus on those errors instead of investing themselves in your protagonist's issues.

Similarly, if your line spacing, margins, indentations, scene headings, and dialogue don't conform to the same rules *every professional script* uses, readers will sigh deeply and throw your script into a pile destined for the dumpster out in the alley.

Here's a cruel truth: Nobody actually _wants_ to read your script.

There's just so much else to do during the day. Answering emails. Checking social media. Going to lunch. Haircuts. Gym workouts. Dog walking. *Anything* but reading your script.

But...maybe your script is the one that actually "has something." Maybe your script is so good that the reader can't put it down until FADE OUT. Maybe your script is so wonderful that it has the potential to generate some serious interest from producers, studios, financiers.

It's the promise of something "so wonderful" and the fear of missing out on a great script that becomes a hit TV show or a box-office winner that briefly and immediately compels producers, managers, agents, actors, and studio execs to open the cover of your script and at least give it a moment of attention.

But that moment is just that...a moment. Pull the reader out of that moment with lousy formatting or spelling-grammar-punctuation errors, and the moment—*your* moment—is lost.

Everyone who reads your script will have other scripts waiting (begging) to be read. Give your reader any excuse to set your script aside, and they'll take it.

Proper formatting isn't just a choice you make or not. **It's an essential requirement.**

We tell stories because we have a hollow place in our heart. You fill it by finding yourself in the stories you tell.

—Guillermo Del Toro
(*The Shape of Water*)

Robert L. McCullough

Preface

This is, in essence, a classic "how-to" book...but if you're at the stage of worrying about—or wanting to be reassured about—your script's formatting, I'll assume you already know the difference between protagonist and antagonist and why that difference is kind of important when it comes to a marketable screenplay.

But if that's the kind of thing you need help with, I'd suggest you take a look at one of the earlier books in this series (*Stop Screwing Around and WIN Your Next Screenplay Contest* or *Stop Screwing Around and Write a Screenplay that SELLS*).

As the co-founder of several well-regarded screenplay competitions where we see upwards of 500 feature film screenplays and TV pilot scripts each month (many of which I personally read), the Numero Uno mistake we see writers make is submitting work that is not properly formatted.

At *The Santa Barbara International Screenplay Awards* and *The Wiki Screenplay Contest,* we always read every page of every script entrusted to us for appraisal. We read every page, even when a script is improperly formatted or replete with typos and grammatical errors, simply because we believe in writers and we have total respect for the tremendous commitment, energy, and discipline it takes to go from FADE IN to FADE OUT.

Part of our job is to do far more than pass judgement on scripts submitted to us; we're here to help writers fix problems and improve their work to the point that it's actually at the professional and marketable level.

That's the fundamental purpose of this small book: to help you present yourself and your work as *professional.*

Writing scripts is not easy, and nobody ever sets out to write a bad one. But when a writer ignores the rules of formatting, that's exactly what they're doing: setting out to write a script that the vast majority of readers will cast aside well before they come to know and love your characters or become enthralled with your brilliant story.

I see a lot of good writers with the potential for creating wonderful movies and TV shows who suffer repeated rejection and frustration simply because their work is poorly formatted or because they haven't carefully proofread their work.

I don't want you to be one of them. I want you to write brilliantly...and to keep your readers turning pages without even noticing your formatting.

>>PLEASE NOTE:
This is a book about *screenplay* formatting. Movies. Nothing else.

This is not a book about the various complexities, variations, and forms of formatting television scripts.

Having written and sold over 300 produced TV scripts, I'm happy to share those guidelines with you...but that's another book.

Robert L. McCullough

Every work of art is a synecdoche, there's no way around it. Every creative work only represents an aspect of the whole of something.

–Charlie Kaufman
(*Eternal Sunshine of the Spotless Mind; Adaptation; Being John Malkovich*)

Robert L. McCullough

Acknowledgements

There have been many fine writers and producers (Bruce Lansbury, Bruce Geller, Earl Hamner, Aaron Spelling, William Goldman, Stephen J. Cannell, George Stevens, Jr., Gene Roddenberry, Jackie Collins, Robert & Barbara Taylor Bradford) who have taught me the art and craft of screenwriting; I'm in debt to them all.

This book would not have been possible without the help and insights of the best story-teller I know: my wife, Suzanne Herrera-McCullough.

As the co-founder of _The Santa Barbara International Screenplay Awards_, _The Wiki Screenplay Contest_, and _The Diverse Writers Outreach Awards_, her relentless dedication to showing writers the path to success never ceases to inspire me.

If you get anything out of this book, it's thanks to her.

Robert L. McCullough

I don't think writers are sacred, but words are. They deserve respect. If you get the right ones in the right order, you can nudge the world a little.

–Tom Stoppard
(*Shakespeare in Love*)

Robert L. McCullough

1. Stay in the Lane

Some writers can crank out a feature screenplay in a couple of weeks. With a solid outline, I've actually written full-length feature first drafts in a week, and full-hour television episodes in two days. (Part of my secret is that I got the best grade in my high school typing class, so I can hit computer keys almost as fast as I can speak.) Of course, to write that quickly, I don't eat much or take a bathroom break until the *very* last minute...which would not be my lifestyle recommendation.

Less compulsive writers generally take months to complete a solid working draft of a screenplay. Procrastinators generally and predictably take much longer.

In the real world—not in the community college screenwriting classes where professors who themselves have likely never sold a single piece of their own writing set artificial deadlines for students to stress over—nobody cares how long it takes you to *write* a script. You won't get a gold star for writing a script quickly...or be penalized for taking your sweet time.

There's simply no way for a script reader to appreciate those long nights you lay awake thinking about a scene or a line of dialogue, or to know how many days you sat butt-numb and staring at a blinking cursor waiting for a neural synapse to create the logic behind your characters' responses to the problems you've created for them.

You may have required the attentions of a chiropractor to deal with the sciatica you've suffered coming up with the perfect plot twist...but nobody— least of all a professional reader at any level in the industry will feel an ounce of empathy, sympathy, or pity.

So, if you're inclined to get a tattoo, start with having this lettered on your forearm: nobody cares how hard your script was to write.

All the reader of your script cares about is how much work it's going to be *for them* to get through it.

Your job: make the reader love your script (and you). You do that by making it *as easy as possible* for the reader to do his/her job.

Remember that regardless of who the reader may be, whether they're a contest reader, manager, agent, studio producer, development executive, or movie star, they don't *really* want to read another script. But they *must read another script* in the hope and expectation that they'll find material they want to work with (and pay you for). They all need something that will demonstrate their ability to pick the wheat from the chaff...and they need a script they *love* in their hands to justify all the work that goes into turning that script into a commercially viable entertainment product.

As soon as your reader opens your script, you want them liking it...and they'll only like it if it's "easy" to read. That doesn't mean you need to write in *Dick-and-Jane-see-Spot-run* syntax or vocabulary, but you do need to speak in the "language of screenwriting" with industry-standard terminology and formatting.

Why? Because readers expect to read your script at the rate of one minute per page or less. That should translate to a minute or less of *screen time* in the finished film.

Compound that with the fact that since the advent of MTV in the 1980s our cultural attention span has dwindled significantly. That phenomenon affects us all; how long will you watch a YouTube video without looking at the right-hand column wondering what else could be more interesting?

In the world of TikTok, text messages, and Instagram, we're all prone to frequent attacks of Attention Deficit Syndrome.

Your readers are no different, so your script must read *quickly*. If it doesn't, they'll be checking their email inbox sooner rather than later.

Your attention to the details of formatting, then, must begin on Page One. Everything must flow from the very first lines of your script with no format tricks or surprises.

Developing and producing television and feature film projects is an arduous, time-consuming and highly competitive business with extreme consequences for either success or failure. Write or produce a highly successful movie or TV series, and you could soon be found at the nearest marina shopping for a mega-yacht. Conversely, fail to write a hit or produce a box-office winner and you can quickly find yourself filing for unemployment benefits.

How competitive is this writing and producing game? Hollywood is like the Roman Coliseum where gladiators fight to the death and only the strongest (or the very best scripts and most tenacious writers) survive.

Maybe that's a little hyperbolic-gruesome...so let's think of your reader as a Formula One race driver. Competitive, impatient, addicted to speed. When a reader opens the cover of your script, they're sliding into the cockpit of the beautifully engineered vehicle you've created and they're expecting to be able to cross the finish line in the shortest possible time. They'll be going *fast* and your script had better be up to the task.

It's all about speed at this point. Flat out down the straightaways with zero distractions as readers head through the twists and turns of your story.

But if "minor" things like formatting irregularities or oddly unclear stage directions or unusually clunky time transitions suddenly appear on the track in front of them and they're forced to swerve to avoid confusion, your script could well hit the metaphorical racetrack's hay bales and crash and burn.

Everyone in the business of finding scripts to produce looks at *a lot* of material. With only so many hours in the day, that means fast, efficient, productive reading. Anything that gets in the way of that is quickly filtered out, rejected.

That's where "industry standard" formatting is of great value, both to you as a writer, and to those reading your scripts. It's a visual language unto itself and one that must be mastered if you hope to communicate your story-telling vision to others.

The size of your vocabulary and your compositional skills notwithstanding, your script needs to be designed for *speed reading*.

The majority of scripts that are optioned, purchased, or put into development only move up the ladder after going through the hands of multiple readers and analysts. (I've never actually heard of a movie going into production from a first draft spec script.) Most of those readers are entry-level assistants serving at the behest of executives or directors and working 10-hour days, tasked with reading multiple scripts and providing some sort of written coverage on a daily basis.

Those readers simply don't have the time to try to figure out what your

script is about or how to interpret
your "creative" formatting.

The key to formatting is to avoid the
unexpected. Don't get tricky or be so
innovative that your reader hesitates
while trying to figure things out.

This is not to say that over the years,
screenplay formats haven't evolved
significantly...because they have.

When I first began reading (and trying
to write) scripts, it was difficult to
even get your hands on anything that
had already been produced or was in the
pre-production pipeline. Studios and
production companies treated script
drafts as though they were state
secrets, only to be seen by "insiders"
attached to the development or
production teams.

Today, practically every film or
television script since *Citizen Kane* or
Twilight Zone is available online. Take
a look at some of those earlier scripts
and you'll see a lot of formatting
devices that are simply no longer in
vogue and will be seen as complete
distractions by contemporary readers.

Even the screenplays for the most well-respected classics like *Apocalypse Now*, *Taxi Driver,* and *Butch Cassidy and The Sundance Kid*—which may remain highly entertaining as examples of dynamic story-telling and memorable characterizations—are formatted a bit anachronistically when compared to the expectations of today's readers.

It must be kept in mind that your scripts will be among many...a veritable *stack* of material sits on the desk of every manager, agent, and producer today. They simply don't have the time for reading scripts that depart from the current formatting norms.

We're going to quickly define those norms here. Deviate from them...drift out of the high speed lane of today's writers and readers...and you'll be in danger of hitting those hay bales.

Robert L. McCullough

When I read a book or hear a story, whether it's over the campfire or in a darkened theater, I just want to feel that I'm not alone. I want to see myself in other characters, and I want to relate to them.

–Bryan Woods
(*A Quiet Place*)

Robert L. McCullough

2.Your Best Friends

We all need a friend now and then. As a screenwriter concerned about formatting your work to give it the best chance of success, you have two friends you can always depend on.

These are the kind of friends who may lurk in the shadows, but they are truly your allies in the street fight of your screenwriting career.

These two friends can help you increase your chances of being the last writer standing. Refuse their help and you'll very likely wind up face-down at your desk with a reader's knife in your back as your dead-as-a-doornail script gets tossed into the dumpster out back.

The friend who will help you produce a script that puts readers at ease and gives them confidence that the rest of their day will go well without discovering a new cure for insomnia is...

White space.

Blank. White. Space.

Remember: readers today have too many scripts to read and too little time to read them. They need to read *quickly*.

That means your script needs to be a "fast read," and the one thing that slows down any script reader are great big blocks of text.

Remember those high school textbooks that had you nodding off in History class? The ones with long paragraphs filled with names, dates, and endless biographical details explaining in grim detail how Abraham Lincoln--or worse yet, King Louis XIV--dealt with political and economic currents of his time? (I nearly put myself to sleep just writing that sentence.)

Keep those paragraphs in mind...and *never write one* in your scripts.

30

Break action sequences up.

Hit the return key frequently.

I know, I know. That sounds "tricky" and manipulative. But contemporary screenwriting requires a certain verbal economy that should translate to the way your words *appear on the page*.

Your job is to artfully force the reader's eyes to race down the page. The challenge is to tell a story while creating a fluid, dynamic, fast-paced reading experience that *compels* the eyes down the page.

Make your script *move* by manipulating the visual impact of the words on your pages.

Over the years of conducting our screenplay competitions and helping writers to improve their chances of commercial success, we've learned a lot about how industry gatekeepers actually read scripts.

They *scan* before they read.

A glance at the first capitalized scene slug tells them generally where the story begins and what time of day it is.

Then their eyes go directly to the first several lines of dialogue.

But wait...what about that first block of stage directions...those flowing sentences that are so artfully composed and elicits such a "feeling" that they could well be the opening paragraph of a best-selling literary masterpiece?

Nobody cares. They're not going to read anything more than two or three lines, and those lines had better be succinct and *to the point*.

And now your other friend steps out of the shadows:

Brevity.

Your favorite author list might include Emily Bronte and Herman Melville, and you may have a deep and abiding background in comparative literature and a shelf full of published novels bearing your name as author, but when it comes to reading your screenplay *nobody cares*.

Readers only care about plunging headlong into your story, meeting your characters, and finding out who they should be rooting for as quickly as possible.

The last thing today's readers want is to be "educated" or lectured to about anything. There is only one thing they expect from reading your script:

To be *entertained*.

To entertain your readers, you need to "show" them your movie in as few words as possible.

Your screenplay is not a novel. Weigh it down with florid prose, uncommon vocabulary, or rambling sentence structure and you will quickly lose your reader.

Remember, you're competing with the reader's email inbox, a ringing phone, and the urge to check this minute's Twitter feed. You don't want to

distract readers with heavy, florid
dialogue or lengthy descriptions.

As a screenwriter, you're akin to an
architect designing a complex urban
skyscraper. Your script is actually
blueprint for getting that highrise
built from the ground up. That
blueprint will ultimately become the
guiding document for all the engineers,
contractors, steel workers, craftsmen,
and laborers who do the actual work of
constructing the edifice of your
dreams.

Everyone on that construction force—
just like the hundred-plus members of
your movie's cast and crew—needs to
know as specifically as possible
exactly what they need to do to bring
your vision to the screen.

That doesn't mean you should make the
cinematographer read pages of rolling
prose describing the reflected glow of
a sunrise in your heroine's eyes or
that you should indicate every
inflection in a character's voice.

Over-describing in stage directions or
dialogue only indicates your lack of
trust in the professionals you hope to

engage with your material. People in the film and entertainment business may not all be PhDs (in fact some of the most successful people in front of and behind the cameras I've worked with barely graduated high school...and many didn't), but none of them are stupid.

They've read scripts before. They get the jokes. They understand the visual medium. They love a good story and they want good characters who generate an emotional investment.

But everyone also knows a bad script when they see it: overwritten, preachy, excessively descriptive, filled with camera angles and instructions to actors, and improperly formatted.

White space. Brevity. The best friends for any screenwriter.

Robert L. McCullough

36

All good, clean stories are melodrama, it's just the set of devices that determines how you show or hide it.

–Baz Luhrmann
(*The Great Gatsby; Moulin Rouge!*)

Robert L. McCullough

3. First Impressions

I magine a doting mother sending out invitations to her daughter's wedding.

Weddings are expensive and generally involved plenty of advance planning. But this mother is insanely frugal and maybe time is short. So she quickly scrawls the names of the bride and groom on Post-its, stuffs them into yellowed envelopes taken from the Motel 6 she stayed at long ago on a college road trip and mails them out to her guest list with five-year-old stamps she finds in the bottom of her kitchen junk drawer and they arrive in your mailbox "postage due."

I don't know about you, but that's not a wedding for which I'd be putting on a clean shirt.

First impressions matter. A lot.

Today's technology has made the dissemination of your screenplay digitally convenient, but there are those occasions when having a hard copy of your script in hand is appropriate.

It's dwindling, but there is still demographic of industry professionals who find reading scripts on a laptop screen to be a complete eye-strain nuisance. Giving written notes on a screenplay in PDF format poses plenty of problems...particularly for those who only use a computer to check their bank balance or to read emails.

Sitting in the bright sun poolside at The Beverly Hills Hotel while reading a script on a laptop screen simply isn't practical. Not only will SPF 50 sunscreen lotion ruin a keyboard, but the monitor glare alone demands that the script be printed, bound, and in one's hands.

So yes, you'll undoubtedly write your script on a computer (hopefully with the help of the right software program—more about that later)and you'll save your final draft in a PDF file that you can send out to the world with the push of a button.

But the time will come when you'll want a hard copy for those folks sipping piña coladas and taking meetings with writers under the striped canopies of reservation-only poolside VIP cabanas.

Look and Feel

When those folks pick up your script, they make two very quick assessments.

The first assessment they make is holding it in their hand for a very brief moment...*weighing* it. Through their extensive experience, they know that a screenplay of 120 pages (anything more and you'd better have written *Gone with the Wind* meets *War and Peace*)written on standard 3-hole punch 20 lb. bond will weigh in at approximately 1.2 pounds. You can print your script out on 30 lb. bond paper, but the weight of those 120 pages will go up accordingly. That might feel "impressive," but it won't *be* that impressive and will instantly make the reader suspect the script is overlength and overwritten. Not the impression you want to make before they've even read your title page.

To make the second snap judgement, your reader will simply fan through the pages. Not reading a single word, but scanning the pages looking for long blocks of text, either in stage directions, action pieces, or dialogue blocks. If the reader spots unbroken paragraphs that resemble a freshman college history textbook without enough of the aforementioned "white space" to make the reading go quickly and comfortably, your script might be well be set aside to be read at a (much) later date.

You don't want to give your reader *any* reason to toss your script into the always-growing pile of rejects; the mere first-glance feel or appearance of a hard-copy script can prevent that from happening.

Because you've most likely written your script using a professional software program (please don't write your script in Word or TextEdit or Notes) that will easily convert your work into a locked PDF file, you'll often be sending it off to several prospective producers, managers, agents, or development execs as a digital file attached to an email.

As efficient and pain-free as that often feels, keep in mind that your formatting still matters. A lot.

When a professional opens your email attachment, they may not be able to hold your script in their hands, but they'll certainly look at the bottom of the document window and catch a glimpse of your page count.

Covers: Plain and Simple

Secondly, they'll simply be looking at the cover page of your script and making an instantaneous second-level judgement that can potentially mark you as an amateur, which will obviously affect their evaluation of all that follows.

Your cover page should appear completely "standard" in every way. Anything that makes it stand out in that pile of scripts on the reader's desk will not be helpful to either you or the reader.

Plain white cardstock...if you must.
Simple 20-30-lb. bond is the true
industry standard and is perfectly
acceptable.

Everything on your title page and on
your script pages should be in Courier
12-point font.

Only four things should appear on your
title page:
1. The title
2. Written by (your name)
3. The date of this draft (which
   should be recent)
4. Your contact information (how they
   can reach you to tell you how
   brilliant your work is)

Keep the layout straightforward and
easy to read at a glance:

- Title of the script in ALL CAPS,
  centered horizontally one-third
  down the page.

- "Written by" double-spaced below
  the title.

- Your name on the next line down.
  If written by a team, an ampersand
  (&) connects them.

- Your contact details (agent's
  name/info, your email address):
  left corner margin, three lines
  from the bottom margin, single-
  spaced, unjustified. I personally
  don't recommend including your
  phone number or home address.

Avoid the temptation to embellish your
script cover in any way. Of course, a
gigantic, bold font might convey the
immense drama swirling around your
charismatic characters...or it might
give the impression that you're *selling*
instead of *telling* your story.

Likewise, don't use day-glo colored
cover stock to attract attention as
though you're worried your reader might
misplace your script or be unable to
find it under all those boring scripts
sitting on his desk.

Maybe you've found a great logo...or
you've created original artwork...or
you have a photo representing the
pivotal scene in your screenplay.

Wouldn't it be great to put that on the cover page, if only to whet the reader's appetite for the incredible story that must lie just beyond that cover page?

No, it wouldn't. It would be a complete turn-off and would instantly earn a huge sigh from your readers who realize they have yet another piece of amateur-time writing to plough through.

Copyright? WGA Registration?

I know what you're thinking: "But what about copyright notices...or my WGA registration?"

Fuggedaboudid.

First of all, filing a copyright with the U.S. Patent and Copyright Office or the Library of Congress is expensive. It's also not necessary because under current copyright law, as soon as you put your name on an original literary work, you *become the copyright owner*.

I'm not saying you shouldn't register your script with the Writers Guild of America-West. It only cost $10, and for a period of five years it does effectively establish the completion date of your original work. It's valuable evidence when you go to court to file multiple lawsuits against all those producers and studio heads who have ripped off your screenplay and every line of your brilliant dialogue.

Unfortunately, registering your script and paying the fee to do so doesn't prevent others from using the identical title, exploiting a similar storyline, theme, or characters. And since most feature films take more than five years to go from script to screen, you'll undoubtedly need to renew your registration at some point as well.

So here's my point: WGA registration isn't a negative, but it's only "evidentiary" when you wind up in a court of law. And putting a copyright or WGA registration notice on the cover of your script generally marks you as a paranoid amateur who just might have a litigious streak...and nobody wants to be in the same room with a writer who has his lawyer on speed dial.

As an aside—and this is touched upon in my very concise book *Stop Screwing Around and Write a Screenplay that SELLS*—neither professional managers, agents, or studio executives are in the business of ripping off writers. There are simply too many good scripts circulating for anyone to get involved with material that might put them at the wrong end of a subpoena.

Nobody wants to steal your script because nobody likes lawyers and it's the best way to kill one's reputation in the business. Everyone simply hopes it's the best script they've ever read.

So don't put "Registered with the WGA" or "Copyrighted" on the cover of your script.

Keeping it all together

Your hard-copy script pages—printed on 3-hole punch paper—need to be held together in some fashion.

It might make all kinds of sense to have them stapled, spiral-bound, screw posts, or plastic comb binding.

Don't do it.

Industry tradition—perhaps motivated by the old school use of photo-copying—calls for the use of heavy-duty brass fasteners...but only in the top and bottom holes of your 3-hole paper. Why just two fasteners when there are three holes? If you know, please drop me an email and explain! (Save the brass?)

I know, it seems irrational for a reader to judge your script using such petty criteria. You'll get no argument from me, but knowing what is "accepted practice" and then conforming to those guidelines will go a long way toward putting your readers in the right frame of mind when they pick up your script.

3-hole 20-23 lb. bond

No "special" fonts.

No graphics.

No warnings of protected rights.

Brass fasteners (two).

Then...make your script cover look like this and you're off to a great start:

YOUR AMAZING STORY

Written by

You Amazing Writer

Contact: YourName@youremailaddress.com

We're inundated all the time with so many things that are based on other existing properties or superhero movies. It's just about finding new stories to tell.

–Scott Beck
(*A Quiet Place*)

Robert L. McCullough

4. The Nitty-Gritty

It all starts with Page One.

Whether you've sent your script via email in PDF file format (the *only* digital format, please)or you've managed to get a hard copy into the hands of a reader, the first page of your script does more than just start to tell your story; it informs the reader either: a) you're a rank amateur with no clue about how to present your work or b) what you've written just might be worth more than a perfunctory glance.

The first page of your script can immediately make the reader regret opening your script...or it can help them relax with the realization that you at least understand the rules of professional formatting.

We were all raised with the well-intentioned warning that "you can't judge a book by its cover," but this is a case where—unfair as it may seem—what you've written will *certainly* be judged by both your cover and your first page.

Just like your cover page, your first should set the pattern for all that follows by conforming to some technical typographical rules. Violate them because you think you've got some cool tricks to make things look "even better" and your reader will soon be checking their voicemail instead of reading page #2 of your script.

One side only

At the risk of pointing out the obvious, your script should be printed on only one side of each sheet of paper.

Save the trees, I know. But this is about contemporary professional screenplay formatting, not forestry management. Yes, you could save a lot of paper (60 sheets in a 120-page script)by printing on both sides of the paper, but <u>don't do it</u>. You'll only make your script feel skinny and seriously annoy your reader while giving the impression that your script reads more slowly than it actually might.

One side of the page. Only. Ever.

Type font

The several choices of font provided in screenwriting software can be very tempting. (I personally have an infatuation with comic sans; it just seems so..."friendly.") This is a temptation that must be overcome at all costs. *Any* font other than the one you see on these pages (fixed-pitch Courier) is to be avoided.

Yes, you *could* write your screenplay in the eminently readable Arial font, but doing so will only make your reader wonder why you stubbornly failed to follow modern professional formatting guidelines.

You'll occasionally have phrases or passages in your script that require emphasis. Occasionally. More than one or two emphatic expressions on a page quickly becomes tiresome, so be conservative in this regard. To give a word or phrase the desired emphasis, underline rather than *italicize* (note that *italics* are somewhat less emphatic and eye-catching than underlines).

Be judicious in your emphatic writing; it becomes very distracting when a page is littered with underlines. Likewise, do not **bold** anything. If underlining doesn't give sufficient emphasis to the reader, then the writing itself should be looked at because you're probably using awkward syntax or poor sentence structure.

Page numbers, headers, footers

Whatever screenwriting software you use, you'll have options about where to put page numbers and how you can fill your header (that space above your top margin) and footer (that space below your bottom margin) with all kinds of wonderful information.

Ignore those options.

There should be no page number on your first page.

All subsequent pages are numbered sequentially in the upper right corner of the header, aligned with the right margin, 3-4 lines from the top, beginning with the number 2, followed by a period in the same Courier font as the script itself. Nothing else should appear in the header. Don't use "Page" in front of the page number. (That's just an extra word on the page, and since we want our script to be a "fast read"...)

Leave your header and footer alone. They look fine—even better—when empty (remember "white space"?) There is no need to remind the reader of the title of your script or your name, or to indicate the date of your draft; it only becomes a visual and completely unnecessary distraction.

Put the TITLE of your script on the first page. Centered, 4-6 lines down from the top, in ALL CAPS. Like this:

<u>REDEEMER</u>

FADE IN

EXT. CARIBBEAN MEXICO COASTLINE - HIGH AERIAL

<u>SUPER: TAMAULIPAS STATE, MEXICO. MARCH 2011</u>

ROCKET DOWN to CIUDAD SAN FERNANDO, MEXICO - AERIAL

over a population of 30,000. KEEP MOVING to the
countryside and

LA JOYA RANCH

in the distance. Isolated. SUVs and armed sentries. PULL
BACK TO REVEAL

FOUR MEN

surveilling the ranch. Binos and scopes. Plainclothes.
Kevlar vests. Armed to the teeth.

RAFAEL TOBIAS, 35, a likeable, careful Mexican Federal
cop.

JASON MORAN. Confident. Irreverent. It's his operation.

BILLY LARSON, TIM CONNORS. Guys you want on your side.

These three could be early-30s surfers looking for a good
point break. Don't be fooled. These dudes are bad-ass DEA
agents.

TOBIAS

whispers to Moran:

                    TOBIAS
          Another time, eh?

MORAN studies the scene below, glances to Larson and
Connors with

                    MORAN
          Long way to come for nothing.

Connors and Larson grin. Cowboys. Ready to rock.

                    CONNORS
          Ya think?

It's long been customary to begin your script with FADE IN on the far left margin two lines above the heading of a script's first scene.

That blank space between those words and your first scene gives the appearance of a wee bit more "white space," but FADE IN is often omitted with today's frequent use of "cold opens" wherein the writer wants to throw the reader immediately into the middle of an action sequence.

In practice, of course, the majority of today's feature films don't "fade in" from black at all; they simply cut into the first shot of the picture.

Likewise, the use of FADE OUT at the conclusion of a script is traditional practice, but is used less frequently today as movies simply cut to black before end credits roll.

Let's call this "a writer's choice" which might very well depend on your need to add or reduce page count, if even by a half-dozen lines of white space.

Margins and page timing

A script of 120 pages is expected to "play" onscreen in 120 minutes. The same script—if every word on the page is read at a normal pace—should read in the same time frame. A maximum of two hours of reading for a two-hour movie.

A wide variation in these ratios indicates that a script is either overwritten or underwritten. The need for consistency comes when budgeting and scheduling production based upon the words on the page.

Imagine a 70-page script envisioned by the writer as a two-hour film and filled with sequences describing battlefield action. There would be no way for a producer to predict the cost of the overall production unless those battlefield sequences are presented in a page count that reflects the number of minutes of expected screen time.

Proper formatting becomes essential to avoid those issues, and requires adherence to specific margin settings for your pages. With the use of today's screenwriting software, a writer no longer needs a slide rule or

a series of tab stops on a typewriter
or in a word processing program. But
even the most basic software allows
writers to adjust and "fudge" their
settings and to thereby reduce or
increase a script's page count without
adding or subtracting verbiage.

Making those adjustments won't fool any
experienced reader or industry
professional, so abide by these hard-
and-fast document settings, using
standard paper size (always!) of 8.5
inches by 11.0 inches (21.5 cm X
27.9cm)

Top margin
1.0" On all but the first page of a
script, the first line of your text
(Scene slug or stage direction
continued from a prior page)should
appear seven lines from the top (bottom
of the header.

Bottom margin
1.0" is standard, but somewhat
flexible, depending on page break
requirements. You don't want to have a
scene slug dangling like an "old maid"
with no stage direction visible under
it. In that case, your bottom margin

may be as much as 1.3" or—if there is
only a single line of action to follow
below the scene slug—as little as .8"

When you have a scene continuing after
the bottom of a page, don't start
throwing in CONTINUED at every
opportunity. Not only does it simply
clutter up your pages with a bunch of
extraneous "technical" jargon, but it
begs the obvious. Movies, by their very
one-scene-after-another nature, are
constantly "continued." CONTINUED is
only appropriate in a parenthetical
under the character name above dialogue
when dialogue is interrupted by a page
break. Avoid them whenever possible.

Action/stage directions:
6" wide. Left margin: 1.5". Right
margin: 1.0" (the left margin is wider
to make room for those three holes and
brass brads).

Dialogue:
3.3" wide. Left margin: 2.9". Right
margin: 2.3"

Character name/cue:
3.3" wide. Left margin: 4.2". Right
margin: 1.0"

Parenthetical:
2.0"wide. Left margin: 3.6". Right margin: 2.0"

Transitions:
1.5"wide. Left margin: 6.0". right margin: 1.5"

Element	Left Margin	Right Margin	Width
Action	1.5	1.0	6.0
Dialogue	2.9	2.3	3.3
Character Cue	4.2	1.0	3.3
Parenthetical	3.6	2.9	2.0
Transition	6.0	1.0	1.5

We've all been tempted to add a few tenths or an inch to those numbers... or to shave a decimal point here or there. Not only will that throw off any future script timing, but narrower margins—whether in stage directions or dialogue—will be instantly recognized for what they are simply because they drag the reader's eyes too far to the left or right, forcing the reader to spend more time on each page.

Not a good thing when we're hoping to make our scripts "a fast read."

Line breaks & spacing

When always using Courier or Courier Screenplay font, be sure your setting is "fixed pitch." Yes, this might make your script appear as though it was written on a 50-year-old manual Remington typewriter, but any other setting might (or the use of "Courier Thin" make it appear as though you're using proportional letter spacing in an attempt to slyly cram more words on a line than would be standard.

Use standard pica line spacing of six lines per vertical inch. Don't get clever by adjusting your line spacing. That will only make your writing appear "dense," more difficult to read, will certainly make everything read more slowly (see "brevity" above).

It might seem like a minor point, but after every period (.), hit your space bar twice. Double space after periods. When you separate sentences with two spaces, you're creating imperceptible "white space" (a good thing, remember), and you're making it easier on your reader's eyes. The same is true of colons (:), of which we hope there are few in the script. But when they do appear, double space before the following word.

I promise, this is the last time:

White space.

Brevity.

Avoid clutter.

Robert L. McCullough

There are a million ideas in a world of stories. Humans are storytelling animal. Everything's a story, everyone's got stories, we're perceiving stories, we're interested in stories.

–Richard Linklater
(*Before Sunrise; Boyhood*)

Robert L. McCullough

5. Scene Slugs & Stage Directions

Because of the way movies are produced and assembled—one scene at a time and with rare exceptions completely out of order from the way the story is told—they're broken down on the script page in individual scenes.

Scene slugs

It doesn't matter if there is any action called for in a scene, or if it's just two people talking on the phone or a single character lying on his back staring at the ceiling and mumbling to himself. We always need to know a few things before the action starts or before characters start speaking.

The scene slug (aka "scene heading")
gives the reader three pieces of
information that immediately inform
what follows in the scene itself.

Where.

The reader needs to know <u>where</u> the
scene takes place. This information is
critical to our understanding of the
setting where things happen (and it's
essential information for the folks who
need to find locations or build sets).
This element will always tell us if
we're "interior" or "exterior" at a
particular location. The abbreviations
"INT." or "EXT." are used. Never spell
out the complete word. Use the period
after the abbreviation with only one
space after the period.

If you've written a sequence that moves
quickly from an interior to an exterior
in a single, uninterrupted shot,
indicate that movement by using
"INT/EXT" or "EXT/INT" (without
periods). You might also use "TRACKING"
immediately following:

INT/EXT JAIL CELL (TRACKING) — DAY

When.

We also need to know <u>when</u> the scene is taking place from a daylight or nighttime perspective. We might also need to know what year it is, or whether we're in the present moment or in the past. This information is necessary for the reader to understand the chronological sequence of events or to glean information from prior events that will come into play in subsequent scenes.

From a production standpoint, the technical production team needs to know whether the scene takes place when the sun is up or when it's in the dark of night. (Remember, your script is a blueprint which needs to inform production personnel what resources they need to prepare for the shooting of any particular scene.) Unless there is a specific visual to this time of day reference ("DAWN"), time of day is almost always indicated in full caps as "DAY" or "NIGHT".

Avoid the use of things like "THE NEXT DAY" or "LATER THAT NIGHT" or "AT THE SAME TIME". If you need to indicate the passage of time within the same scene or location as the prior scene, you might help the reader avoid confusion with the use of a parenthetical like:

INT. JAIL CELL — DAY — (LATER)

Notice the use of space-hyphen-space between the elements in the slug line. Don't omit them or use periods.

If you want to be sure to mark your script as an amateur effort, throw "CONTINUOUS" around in place of indicating "DAY" or "NIGHT". Using "CONTINUOUS" is an obsolete redundancy that will tell the reader nothing. The very nature of movies and film is that everything is continuous, with one shot following another in a running time continuum. Don't use it. It means nothing and is a long word that will just take up valuable page space.

If your reader needs to be aware of a specific historical (or future) time period, indicate that in parentheses as part of your "where" element:

EXT. ALLEY (ROME, 200 B.C.) — DAY

Once the reader is informed thusly, you don't need to remind us in subsequent scenes, i.e.:

EXT. WINDOW ABOVE THE ALLEY — DAY

If a following scene takes place some time later, don't indicate that in the scene slug. Information like "THE FOLLOWING YEAR" should appear on its own line (in caps) above the scene to which it applies:

TEN YEARS LATER

EXT. ALLEY - DAY

Who/what.

The third element of any scene is <u>who or what</u> the audience will be seeing in its opening moments. What should the camera operator be focused on as soon as the director shouts "action"?

Here's what works; it informs the reader of the three essential points of information for an understanding of the action to follow and it tells the producer exactly what's involved from a production standpoint:

```
EXT. LA JOYA RANCH - NIGHT - FOUR ARMED SENTRIES

man stations, assault weapons slung on backs. Quiet.
Fighting boredom.
```

When you want to focus the reader's
attention to individual elements within
the scene itself, individual slugs can
be abbreviated to include only that
specific element. In the example above,
we know were outside the ranch at night
observing "four armed sentries."

But now we want to focus on each of
those sentries in an individual
onscreen moment. Rather than reminding
the reader we're outside a ranch at
night (the reader already knows that
and will remember it), we simply focus
on <u>what we want the reader to "see"</u>:

```
EXT. LA JOYA RANCH - NIGHT - FOUR ARMED SENTRIES

man stations, assault weapons slung on backs. Quiet.
Fighting boredom.

SENTRY #1

stifles a yawn, then falls like a rock. Connors behind
him, blackjack in hand.

SENTRY #2

Lights a cigarette. Sucks on it, never exhales as Larson
choke-holds him from behind. Cracks his larynx. Lights
out.

SENTRY #3

reacts. Heard something. Turns just as Moran checks his
move, snaps his neck. Quietly lowers him to the dirt,
moves off to

SENTRY #4

who reacts to the o.s. sound, calls out:

                    SENTRY #4
          Jorge? Que pasa--?

CLICK. He turns to face the barrel of Moran's Glock on
the end of his nose.
```

By breaking a sequence up to focus on specific visuals within the sequence, notice what happens: what could have been written as a solid block of text describing the action is broken up by lots of white space which makes for faster reading and happier readers.

That technique allows the reader's eye to race down the page and is made possible only when you introduce a scene with a scene slug/heading that fully indicates the essentials of where, when, who/what.

<u>Triple space</u> between the last line of the previous scene (whether dialogue or stage direction/action) and the following scene slug. Those two blank lines will give your page appearance some breathing room while distinctly separating scenes from one another.

Scene slugs are not "scene numbered" until your script is going into production. If you number each individual scene, the page will appear cluttered and distracting; another mark of the amateur. Scene slugs should not be **bold** or <u>underlined</u>. Those are just more visual distractions.

You might write a scene followed by additional action/dialogue in the same place at a later time.

The one thing you do <u>not</u> want to do is attempt to describe the action of the scene that follows within the scene slug. Keep the scene slug brief. It's merely shorthand to set things up and inform us of those three things: Where. When. Who/what.

Your slug lines can—and should—direct the reader's attention to specific visual elements within a scene.

Breaking up blocks of action/stage directions with "mini-slugs" accomplishes a couple of things: it provides additional opportunity for our good friend "white space" and helps generate pacing for the reader.

<u>Avoid</u>, however, the temptation to "play director" on the page. One of the most common notes we give writers who submit their work for our analysis at *The Santa Barbara International Screenplay Awards* is to <u>trust the director</u> to fully understand the visuals in your script. If you're written your script well, there is never a need for things like "REVERSE ANGLE" or "CLOSE-UP" or "DOLLY IN" or "ZOOM OUT." Not only do such things make the reading very clunky, but they seriously irritate directors and will be the first words edited out of your next draft.

Stage directions

Immediately below the scene slug on your script page is where we let the reader know what's happening as soon as we cut to the scene.

<u>Double-space</u> between the scene slug and what follows. One blank line will further "open" the page appearance and cleanly set off the slug line and what follows.

What follows, of course, tells us what's happening in the scene. A brief description of the setting without repeating the obvious (we already know the location, whether we're inside or outside, and the time of day), and introduction to additional characters in the scene, and an indication of the action among characters.

When characters are introduced to the reader for the first time use ALL CAPS for their name. Use upper and lower case for any subsequent mention of the character name in stage directions.

The same is true for any specific visual elements being introduced for the first time. Sound effects or props that need to be emphasized for the reader can ALSO be highlighted with the judicious use of ALL CAPS.

Use the stage direction to <u>briefly</u> set the scene. Again—and if I'm repeating myself it's because this bears repeating—avoid the use of your "director's vocabulary" to indicate "PAN TO" or "ZOOM" or "DOLLY THROUGH". Indicating camera moves is a certain way to avoid having any director show interest in your material. With few exceptions, your writing should provide sufficient visual clues to indicate what we might see on the screen. Don't indicate camera moves. Let the director have some fun too.

Keep this in mind when writing stage directions: nobody wants to read them. They just want the "gist" of what's going on and then they want to get to what actually matters: the personal interactions between characters.

Write more than three or four lines of stage directions, and 90% of your readers will read 10% of the words. The solution is simple: <u>keep it short and to the point</u>. Stage directions are not the place to wax eloquently or display your amazing command of compound-complex sentence structure.

Edit ruthlessly and work aggressively to eliminate all unnecessary verbiage.

Do not "justify" paragraphs. Yes, it might look very slick, but justified margins can create weird word spacing and make reading more difficult (the one thing you want to avoid). Use left margin justification (just like the paragraphs in this book). If an action element describes something that takes place off-screen, "off-screen" should be abbreviated as "o.s." (in lower case).

Avoid the use of ellipses. An ellipsis consists of three periods. No more, no less. There should be a space between an ellipsis and the text that follows it, but no leading space. An ellipsis does not have any spaces between the periods. Text that is visible onscreen, such as a newspaper headline, words on a sign, a text message, or on a computer monitor, should be set off in quotes.

I think you have to write the film that you want to see, and try to do it honestly.

—Edgar Wright
(*Baby Driver; Ant-Man;*
Scott Pilgrim vs. the World)

Robert L. McCullough

6. Abbreviations

While abbreviations and acronyms can often be either confusing or infuriating, they are frequently used as a screenwriting "short hand."

The accurate use of abbreviations accomplishes two things for you, the screenwriter: it helps to ease and accelerate the reading process for industry professionals familiar with them.

This is a good thing because (I'll keep saying this until we're both blue in the face because it can be the absolute key to your success as a screenwriter) <u>nobody actually likes to read</u> and the easier and more fluidly your script reads, the happier your reader will be. A happy reader is the ultimate goal.

With that in mind, the proper use of certain abbreviations will make life easier for everyone. There are dozens, but here are some of the most common (and expected), all indicated in <u>lower case</u>:

Background (b.g.)
Used when calling the reader's attention to something taking place in the background of a scene that has principal action in the foreground:

Foreground (f.g.)
The opposite situation, where things happening closest to the camera lens need to be highlighted for the reader.

Point of view (p.o.v.)
When you want the reader to "see" what a character is seeing.

Without sound/silent (m.o.s.) When a scene plays silently (an odd adaptation of "mitt-out sound" as once commanded by a director with a distinctively German accent)

Voiceover (v.o.) to indicate narration by an individual not part of a scene

Off-screen (o.s.) to indicate speech or sounds taking place within the scene, but without the source visible (commonly used during phone calls)

As you can see, abbreviations that have been established and are in standard use throughout the industry can help an experienced reader to pick up the necessary cues to enable fast reading.

Think of abbreviations—and much of formatting—as though you're writing a musical score. Full notes, half notes, quarter beats, rests, addagios and all the rest of those notations are part of the *language* of musical composition and interpretation.

Your screenplay is no different; it's a distinctive, language that conveys images, sounds, dialogue, and story in a highly codified way.

Learn the language code and use it!

Robert L. McCullough

*I don't think screenplay writing is
the same as writing. I think it's blueprinting.*

—Robert Altman
(*Nashville, The Long Goodbye, Mash*)

Robert L. McCullough

7. Character Cues & Dialogue

Because your characters are the keys to unlock your story, from a formatting standpoint it's truly important that the reader instantly recognizes who they are, what they're doing in your stage directions and who is saying what in your dialogue blocks.

- A "character cue" is the first indication of who is acting or speaking: the character's *name*. Some guidelines in that regard:
- Keep names brief. First and last names are generally overkill (it takes the reader longer to read two names).
- Your lead characters—protagonists and antagonists—rarely require a last name. First names are more

engaging and identifiable for the reader.

- If a character's name changes somewhere in the script (as in using an alias), remind the reader of the original name by indicating it in parentheses the first time the new/second name is used. Any subsequent identification of that character would simply use the new name.
- When introducing a character for the first time in stage directions, use CAPS. All subsequent uses of that name are in upper-and-lower case.
- When characters have something to say in dialogue, it's always preceded by the character name on the line above the dialogue block in CAPS. <u>Not centered</u> above the dialogue block; the first letter of the name lands 4.2 inches from the left side of the paper. (Centering slows reading, as the length of names will vary and appear to jump all over the page.)
- Never place a colon after a character cue above the dialogue block.
- When the same line of dialogue is being spoken by two characters

simultaneously, use a diagonal (/) to separate the character names.

- Avoid the use of "anonymous" character designations ("Man #1). If a character speaks, he (and the actor playing him) deserve the courtesy and respect of giving him a name. Nothing is more confusing than to read a scene, for example, when several characters are only identified by numbers.

- If a character present in a scene but not visible (i.e., hiding under the bed or on the other end of a phone call) speaks from "off stage", use the extension "(O.S.)" immediately after the name cue above the dialogue block. "(V.O.)" is used when indicating voice-over narration by a character *not in the scene*.

The guiding principle in the use of name cues and character introductions is *clarity*.

Make the reader's job easier by consistently identifying who's in the scene, where they are, and who's speaking.

Dialogue blocks are not centered (although they may look like it at first glance). The left margin of dialogue (left justified) is placed 2.9 inches from the left edge of the page. Other notable standards for dialogue formatting include:

- Don't break a page in the middle of a line (sentence) of dialogue.
- When a page break occurs in the middle of dialogue, add (MORE)in all caps with parenthesis on its own line at the bottom of the page, appearing on the same margin as the character cue above.
  - On the following page, immediately to the right of the character cue/name, insert "cont'd" (in lower case without the quotation marks)one space after the character name.
- All numbers appearing in dialogue are spelled out. No numerals less than one hundred (100) appear in dialogue.
- If a character reads aloud from a text as part of dialogue, indicate this with (reading) on its own line immediately under the character cue.

- Interrupted dialogue—when one character cuts off another's speaking—is indicated with an M-dash (a space followed by double hyphens) with no period.
- When one character interrupts and finishes the line of another, don't use a dash; just begin that dialogue with the first word of the speech.
- If a character's dialogue trails off (an unfinished thought or expression), use an ellipsis.
- Don't use ALL CAPS or italics for emphasis in dialogue. If you <u>must</u> use emphasis (the dialogue itself should inform the actor without typography), <u>underline</u> the words to be emphasized.
- Parallel dialogue—when two characters are speaking at the same time—is indicated with two columns with the left margin of the first dialogue column inset three spaces from the left margin.

"Wrylies" should be avoided as much as possible.

Prior generations of screenwriters, out of apparent disregard for the abilities

93

of actors to properly interpret the intent of dialogue, developed the bad habit of including not-so-subtle "personal directions" or "parentheticals" on the first line under the character cue/name before the actual dialogue begins. This was the writer's way of giving line readings to actors like this:

                    JOHN
            (with a wry smile)
        You can't be serious, Mary.

You can see how those parentheticals came to be known as "wrylies."

Today, where speed of reading is essential and where actors and directors are assumed to accurately interpret proper intonation in well-written dialogue, such things are not generally appreciated or necessary.

Sprinkle wrylies throughout your script and you won't win any friends on the set. It's much more artful to include any hints of interpretation in the stage directions leading up to the dialogue.

94

If it's absolutely essential that you indicate some performance element in the dialogue...

> MARY
> (sobbing uncontrollably)
> You don't love me at all.

...put the left parenthesis 3.6 inches from the left side of the page and keep it short. No complete sentences, no capitalization, no punctuation.

Obviously, any "personal direction" should only apply to the character speaking; nothing should apply to the actions, reactions, or intentions of other characters. The exception would involve the speaker's reaction to other character's actions or dialogue:

> JOHN
> (ignoring her tears)
> If only that were true, my dear.

Whenever a character's dialogue is interrupted by a piece of action/stage direction, and the same character continues speaking, add (CONT'D) one space following the character cue:

                    JOHN (CONT'D)
        But you know I do love you.

Because genuine human speech is rarely
continuously fluent and flowing,
dialogue often requires a moment of
reflection, or a break in speaking.
Rather than use "pause" or "beat",
actors today prefer the most modest of
indications:

                    MARY
        Am I supposed to believe
        that?
                (then)
        I don't suppose I really
        have a choice.

The use of (then) is a gentle way of
indicating the actor should "take a
moment" before continuing. Anything
more and you risk having an actor throw
your script at your head while shouting
"Let me act!" (This actually happened
to me. I ducked and survived to write
another day...but I learned a lesson I
won't forget.)

96

The coming up with ideas doesn't happen when you're trying to think of ideas. I don't know that I ever sit somewhere and think, 'Oh, I have to think of ideas now.' An idea just sort of floats into your brain when you're living your life. It's not like you have 10 ideas a day. If you have two good ideas for a movie in a year, that's amazing.

–Aline Brosh McKenna
(*The Devil Wears Prada*)

Robert L. McCullough

8. Transitions, Titles, and Cool Stuff

H ere's where you get to type all the cool stuff that helps the reader move from scene to scene or "shot to shot" while letting you feel like you're really writing an actual *movie*.

Totally cool...and usually pointless.

Transitions

There was a time when reading a screenplay was a seriously unique experience, and most people had very little experience in the craft. There was also a time when most people read the folios of Charles Dickens as they were published every 90 days for their entertainment.

Those times are long gone. As I've said earlier, today's screenplay reader (whether that's a paid contest reader, literary manager, producer, studio development exec, director, or actor) wants to read your script *quickly*.

Hopefully, everyone who reads your script knows something about how a film is constructed in a series of shots that are stuck together in some sort of meaningful order that tells a story.

In other words, film is just one scene and one shot after another, running past our eyeballs at such a fast clip that it all appears to transpire fluidly.

The closer your screenplay comes to mimicking that effect—one thing after another in an unstoppable sequence of images, words, sounds—the more your reader will feel like it's a *movie* and not just a bunch of typewritten words on paper.

So why would you want to screw that up with anything that distracts the reader from the *experience* of your movie?

That's what transitions are really good at: pulling your reader "out" of your movie.

Not too long ago, when a writer wanted to indicate the end of a contiguous sequence or a break in time/location, they'd insert "CUT TO" between scenes, usually placed on the right side margin:

```
                    SAMANTHA
              Look, all we need is a credible story,
              and we need to stick to it--

      They're suddenly startled by the o.s. SOUND of the DOORBELL
      and we
                                              CUT TO:


      INT. THE LIVING ROOM - TEN MINUTES LATER - SAMANTHA, ANNE,
      AND SHEILA

      are all on the living room couch, facing OFFICER JENNINGS, a
      clean-cut  uniformed cop who makes notes on a small pad:
```

That looks pretty "scripty" but what meaning does it actually convey? Does it tell the reader something they don't know...that we're now moving on to another scene? No. It's simply redundant, pulls the reader's eye off the center line of the page (which is where readers' eyes want to stay), and can consume a ton of valuable space on the page that you might want to retrieve when you find you've written a script that is far too long.

This is not to say that some of the best scripts of all time aren't filled with things like "CUT TO" and "DISSOLVE TO" or (my favorite no-no) "SMASH CUT", but the only screenplay of any real note that is filled with that stuff is William Goldman's 1969 Oscar winner *Butch Cassidy and The Sundance Kid*. That script—which stands at a whopping 185 pages and wouldn't even make it past a studio reader at that length today—has "CUT TO" between nearly *every single scene/shot*. Goldman used that as a device to pull the reader along through pages of run-on sentences and over-description, and in 1969 it was very different.

But this isn't 1969 and you aren't William Goldman. So don't do it.

99% of all transition indicators are simply superfluous. Why write (and take up the space on the page) "CUT TO" when all transitions are by their very nature <u>cuts</u>? Why indeed.

102

If you *must* use a transitional instruction (do so at your own risk, folks), place it 6.1 inches from the left side of the page or you can justify it on the right margin. Only "FADE IN" is ever placed at the left margin. "FADE OUT" is only used at the end of your script and is placed on the right margin, double spaced below the last line of the final scene or line of dialogue.

Titles and other words on screen

Aside from the title of your movie centered at the top of the first page of your script, don't go to the trouble of finding "the perfect scene" where you can tell the director or editor where to "roll credits."

Not only is that superfluous, but it will always be ignored, so why bother to come off like an amateur?

But what about when you need to let the reader/viewer know some critical information that may not be obvious in the playing of the scene? (Remember, your script should be as nearly

103

"visual" as possible, as though the
reader is actually *seeing* the movie.)
When setting up a specific place or
time for the scene that follows, use
"SUPERIMPOSE:" (all CAPS with a
colon)written in the scene slug itself:

EXT. DESERT — DAY — A ROVER

crawls over rocks, kicking up red dust. SUPERIMPOSE: "The
Surface of Mars, 2099"

Don't abbreviate "SUPERIMPOSE" as
"SUPER" or place it above or below the
scene slug/heading. It should follow at
least one sentence of description so we
understand *why* we need to know the
information presented in text on the
movie screen.

The only title you'll want to routinely
include comes when you've finished
telling your amazing story: "<u>THE END</u>".

This is centered, double spaced below
"FADE OUT", in all CAPS and underlined.

Nothing should follow "<u>THE END</u>".

Nothing.

You need time. And that doesn't mean necessarily even working full-time on it itself; it means time to throw some ideas together and let them sit, go off and do something else, come back and see what still feels right.

–Christopher Nolan
(*Inception; The Dark Knight; Dunkirk*)

Robert L. McCullough

9. Flashbacks, Montages, Phone Calls

Because film is a visual medium that allows us to manipulate our perceptions of time and space (after all, nothing we see on the screen is *real*, but we suspend disbelief long enough to let ourselves *believe* that those dancing images are veritably what we're witnessing), taking the reader/viewer either backward or forward in time, there are various and often effective—if not overused—techniques used to accomplish that.

Flashbacks

Flashbacks allow us to provide details of characters' histories, defining

motivations moving forward. Examples of
the effective use of flashbacks are
everywhere: *Casablanca, Sunset
Boulevard, Citizen Kane, Godfather II,
Forrest Gump, Saving Private Ryan,
Titanic*...you get the point. Flashbacks
are so common as to be a part of every
filmmaker's vocabulary simply because
they enable acceleration of storylines
and resolutions.

Perhaps because of the phenomenon of
"cold opens" in today's television
series, filmmakers have begun employing
the technique of opening a movie with a
sequence of pell-mell, completely
unexplained or unmotivated action...all
of which is then made clear to us in
either a flashback or flashforward
immediately following.

The trick is to present your flashbacks
as clearly and *consistently* on the page
as possible.

To do that, simply insert the word
"FLASHBACK" (inside parentheses, all
CAPS, no quotation marks) in the scene
slug, followed by a single blank line
with the stage direction/action lines
on the immediately following second
line:

INT. CASTLE — NIGHT — (FLASHBACK)

DR. EVIL enters, carrying the shrouded
body of his latest victim....

When the flashback scene ends and
we're meant to return to the present
action, you need to indicate that when
the action in that scene concludes
with "END FLASHBACK." (in parentheses
with period) , i.e.:

INT. CASTLE — NIGHT — (FLASHBACK)

DR. EVIL enters, carrying the body of
his latest victim. He sets the corpse
on a massive table, pulls back the
shroud to reveal the face of his twin
brother. (END FLASHBACK.)

Consistency is key here. Avoid
throwing the word "FLASHBACK" all over
the page; no need to make it a right
margin-hugging transition, which only
slows the reading.

Montages

One of the earliest and most useful
film techniques, montages—sequences of

shots or brief scene moments—allow us to shrink time and space...and to keep readers and audiences fully engaged with visuals that do some of the heavy lifting of our story exposition. Filmmakers who know their craft well can artfully employ a series of very brief shots to explain a chain of events or transitional sequences without boring us to death with protracted dialogue exposition.

Rather than detail each of those shots with full scene slugs and repetitive stage direction/action lines, simply indicate "SERIES OF SHOTS" thusly:

SERIES OF SHOTS — DR. EVIL IN HIS LAB
    A) Brushing his dead twin's hair away
       from the face.
    B) Forcing the twin's eye open.
    C) Raising a scalpel.
    D) Cutting into his twin's eye socket.
    E) Holding the eyeball up to the light,
       laughing.

Be careful that the text in each shot wraps beneath and doesn't extend under the letter of the mini-outline. You'll be creating a "hanging indent" with a hard return at the end of each line. (Some screenplay formatting software doesn't do this for you, so you'll need to manually override.)

You don't need to write "End Montage" or anything like that; the reader will know when it ends because your margins will return to normal and your new/following scene slug will be appropriately spaced and placed.

Phone calls

In a contemporary setting, the majority of your characters will have a smartphone in their pockets, so a good deal of story-telling might very well take place while they're talking to each other from different locations. The trick here, as in so much of proper formatting, is to be consistent and make it as easy as humanly possible for the reader to know exactly who is where and to whom they're speaking.

First, establish one location with a brief slug identifying a character *on the phone*:

    EXT. JERRY'S BUILDING — DAY — SUE

    Stands in the doorway, pulls her phone out of her purse, punches a number.

111

Then, show us the recipient of that call:

INT. BEDROOM — DAY — JERRY

is in bed, reacts to his ringing phone, turns away from the blonde at his side, picks up the phone, rubs his eyes.

At this point, add the words "INTERCUT with" followed by the caller's location prior to the first line of the caller's dialogue:

INT. BEDROOM — DAY — JERRY

is in bed, reacts to his ringing phone, turns away from the blonde at his side, picks up the phone, rubs his eyes.

INTERCUT with

EXT. SIDEWALK — DAY — SUE

who suspects nothing.

>   SUE
>   (into phone)
>   Hi. It's me—

>   JERRY
>   (into phone)
>   Oh, yeah. Hey-

                              SUE
                        (into phone)
                    I'm downstairs, thought
                    I'd drop by.
                              JERRY
                        (into phone)
                    Oh, yeah?
                        (then)
                    Actually, I've got an
                    awful headache-

We'll leave Jerry to his own devices at
this point, but notice the use of (into
phone) which makes it very clear that
Jerry isn't talking to the blonde under
the covers, but that he's speaking to
Sue.

Also notice the use of (then) to
indicate a pause in his dialogue as he
scrambles for an excuse to prevent Sue
from walking in and finding him with
the blonde.

Now...what if the blonde had been in
the bathroom when Jerry's phone rang.
Her dialogue would be indicated thusly:

    INT. BEDROOM — DAY — JERRY

    is in bed, reacts to his ringing phone,
    picks it up, rubs his eyes.

                                        113

INTERCUT with

EXT. SIDEWALK — DAY — SUE

who cheerfully suspects nothing.

> SUE
> (into phone)
> Hi. It's me—

> JERRY
> (into phone)
> Oh, yeah. Hey-

> BLONDE (O.S.)
> Who's that, Jerry?

He covers the phone with the pillow.

> JERRY
> Wrong number. Robo call.
> (into phone)
> I was gonna call you,
> But I've got this cold.

When a character who is in the same location and speaks but is unseen (in Jerry's bathroom), indicate "(O.S.)" immediately after their character cue.

Writers often mistakenly use "(V.O.)" in that case, but (V.O.) indicates *voiceover*, which should be reserved for dialogue spoken by a narrator.

114

The cinema that I make is a cinema about people, emotion, humanity, and passion. It's not just about what they struggle through, but what they live for. That's what I love. The music they love, the people they love, the clothing, the hair, and the life that they love.

–David O. Russell
(*Silver Linings Playbook*)

Robert L. McCullough

10. Before You Go

I know.

Formatting. What could be more boring, tedious, and completely beside the point when you've got a script ready to send out to the folks who write the big checks?

But is your script *really* ready? Unless you *know* it's ready, please don't send your scripts out for consideration by any actual industry professionals.

Letting your parents, your significant others, or friends read your script is fine. But if you send a piece out into the real world and it's not *truly* ready, it will be seen as "not quite there yet" and will promptly be dismissed...*forever*.

Once you're sure your script is indeed properly formatted, please take a deep breath and consider once again (I hope it's "once again" and that you've already considered it) the fact that your script might be one of perhaps 1,000 that an individual reader, agent, manager, producer, or studio development exec will read *just this year.*

Keep in mind that there are 999 *other scripts* written by folks just as ambitious and eager as you are. In other words...

This is a blood sport. You are competing for recognition in an industry which "processes" in a single year more scripts than can possibly be financed, developed, or put into production in the next 100 years.

This means your screenplay needs to be **the best in every way.**

You may have the most amazing story ever told...you may have compelling characters facing unique and never-before seen challenges...you may have even written the most clever dialogue ever spoken on screen...

But if your script has more than the occasional—make that _very_ occasional—typo, misspelling, grammatical error, or errant punctuation, you'll be seen as sloppy and possibly unprofessional.

You and your script will be "done." If you don't care about how your script feels, looks, and reads...I promise you this: no professional reader will be remotely interested in reading your script.

So, once you're confident everything is ship-shape, run a spell-check program. Then run another spell-check program. They're free online, and the time it takes to run your script through them is nothing compared to the time it has taken you to write the script.

In your work as a screenwriter, it should become a matter of habit to read the work of others. You can now find complete libraries of produced screenplays online.

Among those myriad screenplays, you'll undoubtedly find outliers and exceptions to all the rules I've laid out for you here. Certainly Christopher

119

Nolan, David Lynch, Quentin Tarantino are among contemporary screenwriters who don't conform to every traditional writing standard.

But you're not them.

You do *not* want your script to stand out from the pack because you've reinvented screenplay formatting. You want your script to stand out from the pack because your writing is simply and undeniably better than anyone has ever had the pleasure of finding on their desk.

Write well. Format accurately.

You'll be far ahead of most everyone out there.

The more a project scares you, the more that probably means it's worth doing.

–Damien Chazelle
(*La La Land; Whiplash*)

Robert L. McCullough

Once More...with Feeling

There's nothing more depressing than seeing a really great script land in the rejection pile because the writer didn't know a few basic things...things I simply can't resist repeating.

You can find the following in _Stop Screwing Around and WIN Your Next Screenplay Contest_ and in _Stop Screwing Around and Write a Screenplay that SELLS_ (available at Amazon), but it's stuff that's too valuable not to repeat here because I want you to have the very best possible shot at getting your screenplay sold...and because I believe in the value of repetition.

Many times a writer will have a terrific script with all of the elements we've dealt with here in place...and then they blow it by doing something lame and patently amateurish (like ignoring proper formatting).

So please do the following to give your script a professional appearance.

- Leave your logline off the cover page. Don't even put your logline on the first inside page. It will simply stop the reader from turning that page because they will "already know what it's all about."

- Use white paper only. Period.

- Keep stage directions simple and short. Long paragraphs of single-spaced ink are a complete turn-off. And do not include camera directions like PAN LEFT or DOLLY IN or RACK FOCUS unless you want a director to line the bottom of his parakeet's cage with it.

- Avoid writing in a literary style. Distract the reader with high falutin' vocabulary, and you'll lose him/her. This is the movie business, not a graduate course in Elizabethan Literature.

- Eliminate any and all technical vocabulary. The use of gratuitous technical terminology will bring the reader to a dead halt. "Gun" is far better than a detailed description of the caliber and rifle barreling.

- Omit any and all redundant or repeated transition slugs. "Cut To" feels really cool to type into your script, but it will quickly irritate your reader.

- Keep any transitions simple and standard. Getting fancy with transitions between your scenes ("RIPPLE DISSOLVE", "LEFT WIPE", "IRIS OUT") is beyond distracting to the reader.

- Don't write what can't be shot. If it can't be shot or translated into words and images on the screen, it doesn't belong in your script.

- Omit any WGA registration or copyright notices.

- Omit any set-character-location lists. (That's not your job.)

- Page numbers go in the upper right header corner on all pages *except* the first page.

- Nothing else should be written in headers or footers.

- Compose in Courier or Courier Screenwriter 12 pt. font only.

- Don't put (CONT'D) or (CONTINUED) at the bottom of any page.

- Do not use scene numbers (until you've sold your script and it's in production...and then it's someone else's job!)

- Do not **bold** slug lines or anything else. I know: Coppola does it a lot...but he's Coppola, okay?

- Do not use italics for emphasis in dialogue. Use <u>underlines</u> only. Infrequently, please.

- Don't include any indication of film credits or title placement (also someone else's job).

- Use scene slugs/headings for each and every scene (it's a script, not a novel).

- Be stingy with "parentheticals" and "wrylies." (Trust the actors and directors.)

- Punctuate accurately. Go easy on the commas and exclamation marks and single space (not double) after periods.

- Use FULL CAPS when introducing characters for the first time only.

- Don't put asterisks (*) anywhere or to indicate omitted scenes or dialogue.

- NEVER self-format in Google Docs or in MS Word. That's crazy-making. Use screenwriting software and make your life a *lot* easier.

- Write frugally. White space is your friend.

- A WGA Registration number might impress *you*, but it tells the reader you don't trust him/her and you're ready to sue anyone who doesn't make your movie. Don't put registration numbers or copyright warnings on your script cover.

- Avoid using artwork on a fancy cover. Professionals simply use a standard piece of paper for their script cover. Three-hole paper held together by two simple brass brads.

- Do not include scene and character breakdowns or set lists. Again, that's someone else's job. Your only job is to tell a compelling story that they simply can't put down until FADE OUT. Nothing more.

Avoiding these mistakes is no guarantee that you'll sell your script, but making these mistakes is a guarantee that you *won't* sell it.

Just for You

You deserve to make rapid progress as a screenwriter. Because you've shown the tenacity to read this far...

When you join us at *The Santa Barbara International Screenplay Awards*, you're entitled to a 35% discount (that's a full $100 saving on Line Notes & Consultation entries) on any contest entry with written feedback. Just use the Discount Code FORMATBOOK when you enter any one of the four annual competitions here.

You'll have a shot at $50,000 worth of annual cash prizes, commemorative trophies, online publicity, and live one-on-one consultations that include script notes just like you'd get in a meeting with any Hollywood producer.

Many of our winners have gone on to serious professional success.

Now it's your turn!

Robert L. McAlloy

129

Robert L. McCullough

About the Author

Robert L. McCullough has more than 300 produced <u>IMDB</u> credits in film and television.

Bob and his wife Suzanne live in Santa Barbara, where they host the celebrity podcast series *Where Hollywood Hides*.

Recognized throughout the industry as experienced writing and producing professionals dedicated to helping new writers bring their work up to the professional level, Bob and Suzanne are the co-founders of *The Santa Barbara International Screenplay Awards*, *The Diverse Writers Outreach Awards*, *The Wiki Screenplay Contest*, and *The Los Angeles International Screenplay Awards*.

Bob holds screenwriting degrees from University of Southern California, the University of Texas, The American Film Institute, and is a Juris Doctorate at

Southwestern University School of Law. An Emeritus Member of Writers Guild of America, his complete credit history is available at IMDB.

Bob can be reached directly via email: info@santabarbarascreenplayawards.com

Stephanie S.
7:38 PM (2 hours ago)

Hi Suzanne and Bob—
I have some wonderful personal news that I'd like to share with you all: as of yesterday,
I have been offered a writing apprenticeship at Netflix Animation on a new television
series! This is a huge step for me, and I'm still a bit shocked (to say the absolute least,
ha!).
Thank you all. You were quite seriously the first people to give me the kind of help I
needed.

Richard M.   Mon, Nov 29,
                                                                                    10:32 AM

Bob:
I want you to know that I just signed with a manager--Kathy Muraviov of The Muraviov
Company. Thanks again for all your help and advice. I owe a lot to you and The Santa
Barbara Screenplay Awards for this boost to my career.

John Cooney

My thanks to everyone associated with the Santa
Barbara International Screenplay Awards. The
feedback and notes I have received, as well as
information imparted to me to me during my
consultation, have been invaluable in helping me
understand what I need to do in order to achieve my
screenwriting goals. Best wishes for continued
success!

**Maria Massei-
Rosato**

Extremely happy with this contest! I signed up for
Line Notes & Live Consultation and received candid
and caring feedback from one of the best in the
business. It's obvious the goal of this contest is to
help screenwriters reach their ultimate potential. And
I am confident the advice I received will help advance
my script.

Robert Deigh

Entered the SBICA competition and ordered Academy Analysis. The coverage was excellent - virtually all actionable suggestions that made the script, the story, and the main characters better. Obvious that the reader read every word. Ended up with an honorable mention in the competition which was very nice too. Purchased coverage can sometimes be hit-and-miss. The SBICA coverage is a hit.

Stephen Colley

An enjoyable contest to enter -- well organized, with clear description and instructions for ease of entry, and on-time reporting and comments. Thank you for a pleasant and useful experience.

Doug Williams

This is without question one of the most supportive, most professional, best-run, high-value competitions out there. Bob McCullough is just terrific -- his comments, insights, and recommendations on my script (which was named Best Feature) have made every page of it better in rewrite. I cannot recommend it more highly. Every competition should be as good as this one.

Show Less

February 2022

🖒 Helpful

Rachael Berman & Chuck Alley

Barbara International Screenplay Awards was a fantastic experience. We received a Quarter Finalist Award and also had the opportunity for a personal Live Consultation with Robert L. McCullough. He took us through a page by page discussion about our script. Bob was very through, honest and drilled down on specifics on how we could improve our writing and our script. It was a Master Class on script writing to say the least. Thank you Bob and thank you Santa Barbara International Screenplay Awards for your recognition of our work.

135

James Kahn

These guys were great. Responsive, personal, great feedback on a first draft that was so useful on completing a rewrite - and rewriting is what it's all about. You don't feel like you're sending your script into the void here. It's not just a contest. It makes your script better.

Tricia Tribble

We are retired, married, newbies to writing screenplays with stories to tell.
Santa Barbara International Screenplay Awards' live insight gave us specific assistance. We have heard this type of advice from others festivals. BUT, we finally we received the coaching that brings our story from the relm of a nice hobby to viability.

Mark Rigoglioso

I received prompt and very professional coverage based on my selection for the contest. Email Communications were always prompt and professional; and I always I felt that I was in the right place at the right time. I was selected for the festival, although I did not receive any awards or special mention. I did receive excellent coverage that helped me to sharpen my script to a very professional level.

Richard Muti

What attracted me to the Santa Barbara awards competition was its promise that my script would be reviewed by industry professionals. They kept their promise, and I am thrilled with the result. Highly recommend.

Maria Massei-Rosato

Extremely happy with this contest! I signed up for Line Notes & Live Consultation and received candid and caring feedback from one of the best in the business. It's obvious the goal of this contest is to help screenwriters reach their ultimate potential. And I am confident the advice I received will help advance my script.

Jayne Cox

I cannot be more grateful to Mr. Robert McCullough for the excellent "Line Notes & Live Consultation" and "Live-Zoom Script Conference" that we had. together. Without question, it allowed me to transform my screenplay into a more professional document. My monetary investment was nothing compared the to time and effort that Mr. McCullough put into reviewing and analyzing my screenplay, page-by-page. It was well worth the investment, as Mr. McCullough delivered more than what he was paid.

Garrison Wells

Great festival and they are wonderful at reviewing your screenplay and communicating with screenwriters
This was my fourth festival and this one was by far the best

Ali Kiani

There are many screenwriting competitions out there, and they keep growing. I believe the quality of an organization's plan for the event is not its name or location but the people who run the event and those who evaluate the scripts. I firmly believe that the Santa Barbara International Screenplay competition readers are not passive young readers but active professionals who work in the industry and care for the art of writing.
Ali Kiani

Rachael Berman & Chuck Alley

Barbara International Screenplay Awards was a fantastic experience. We received a Quarter Finalist Award and also had the opportunity for a personal Live Consultation with Robert L. McCullough. He took us through a page by page discussion about our script. Bob was very through, honest and drilled down on specifics on how we could improve our writing and our script. It was a Master Class on script writing to say the least. Thank you Bob and thank you Santa Barbara International Screenplay Awards for your recognition of our work.

Doug Williams

This is without question one of the most supportive, most professional, best-run, high-value competitions out there. Bob McCullough is just terrific -- his comments, insights, and recommendations on my script (which was named Best Feature) have made every page of it better in rewrite. I cannot recommend it more highly. Every competition should be as good as this one.

Stephen

I am deeply appreciative of the constructive comments that the SBISA judges provided, which have helped me develop a better screenplay. I will enter again.

Duncan Payne

First... Absolutely the best screenwriting experience I've ever had. This is not hyperbole... just the fact. Second... the staff at Santa Barbara International Screenplay Awards could not have been more attentive to my questions. Third... Get the Book... "Stop S******* Around and Win Your Next Screenplay Contest!" It is short, direct, informative and pure gold. No kidding.

If you've been entering screenplay contests, you know how frustrating it can be to fall short of winning.

This little book can change all that.

It's the absolute bottom line, short and sweet.

Stop Screwing Around and WIN Your Next Screenplay Contest!: Your Step-by-Step Guide to Winning Hollywood's Biggest Screenwriting Competitions

10 short no-nonsense chapters show you exactly how to write a screenplay that wins major competitions and attracts serious attention from Hollywood studios and producers.

This book delivers the point-by-point essentials behind every successful screenplay and shows you how to demonstrate the professional expertise that will get your scripts noticed.

$12.49 ON AMAZON

139

rokqueenLA

★★★★☆ **To the point**
Reviewed in the United States on June 1, 2022
Verified Purchase

Good info. Great book for the basics! Helpful

    Helpful   Report abuse

 DianaB

★★★★★ **Excellent Resource**
Reviewed in the United States on February 6, 2020
Verified Purchase

Rob offers an excellent checklist into getting into the top rankings and/or winning reputable screenwriting competitions....
Follow his solid, down-to-earth, no BS advice and you'll be working towards success.. Speaking from experience, I purchased this text after having achieved 'Finalist' status in the Los Angeles International Screenplay Awards 2019. (he's a panel judge) and reading the text, I was able to 'tick boxes' and felt assured I was working in the right direction... .

One person found this helpful

    Helpful   Report abuse

 ZMark

★★★★★ **Essential Info From A Veteran Hollywood Professional**
Reviewed in the United States on June 30, 2019
Verified Purchase

Robert McCullough gives straight, cut to the chase essentials to writing a script that will get noticed and sold. The information is clearly outlined and easy to understand. It's practical application from a veteran Hollywood writer, director and producer. It contains exactly what you need to know to write a successful script and how to do it. This book is a necessity for anyone trying to break into the business. Stop Screwing Around and Write a Screenplay that Sells is THE guide book for anyone serious about being a professional screenwriter.

2 people found this helpful

    Helpful   Report abuse

 Garner Simmons

★★★★★ **McCullough gets it right**
Reviewed in the United States on April 9, 2019
Verified Purchase

Robert McCullough gets directly to the heart of the matter: If you are going to be a successful screenwriter, you need to be able to compete at the highest level. To pretend you can get away with doing less is a cop out. Writing that fails to sell is a waste of your time. McCullough provides a clear-eyed analysis of what it takes to create a viable commercial screenplay, writing that will attract an agent, a producer, director and star. Decidedly a book worth reading and rereading.

7 people found this helpful

Stop Screwing Around and Write a Screenplay that SELLS!

Your Step-by-Step Guide to Writing a Script that Gets Produced

12 short no-nonsense chapters show you exactly how to write a screenplay that immediately attracts the attention of Hollywood Literary Managers, Agents, and Producers...the people who are critical to your screenwriting success.

This book "cuts to the chase" with the point-by-point essentials behind every screenplay that **sells**.

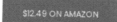

$12.49 ON AMAZON

ZMark

★★★★★ **Essential Info From A Veteran Hollywood Professional**
Reviewed in the United States on June 30, 2019
Verified Purchase

Robert McCullough gives straight, cut to the chase essentials to writing a script that will get noticed and sold. The information is clearly outlined and easy to understand. It's practical application from a veteran Hollywood writer, director and producer. It contains exactly what you need to know to write a successful script and how to do it. This book is a necessity for anyone trying to break into the business. Stop Screwing Around and Write a Screenplay that Sells is THE guide book for anyone serious about being a professional screenwriter.

2 people found this helpful

Helpful | Report abuse

 Garner Simmons

★★★★★ **McCullough gets it right**
Reviewed in the United States on April 9, 2019
Verified Purchase

Robert McCullough gets directly to the heart of the matter: If you are going to be a successful screenwriter, you need to be able to compete at the highest level. To pretend you can get away with doing less is a cop out. Writing that fails to sell is a waste of your time. McCullough provides a clear-eyed analysis of what it takes to create a viable commercial screenplay, writing that will attract an agent, a producer, director and star. Decidedly a book worth reading and rereading.

3 people found this helpful

Helpful | Report abuse

 L. Mccracken

★★★★★ **The Essential Handbook for aspiring screenwriters!**
Reviewed in the United States on May 14, 2019
Verified Purchase

Finally--- a no nonsense guide from a true writer of television and motion picture that will have you up to speed and writing like you knew you were capable of. Bringing over 300 successful scripts to life from the 1970's till now, Robert McCullough has battled and conquered the trenches of how to make a good script great, and get them noticed and sold. What are you waiting for? Stop screwing around and get one! Thanks Bob!

Now that you've read this book...

Shouldn't you be writing?

Robert L. McCullough

Printed in Great Britain
by Amazon